Ten Poems
about Dogs

ex libris

Candlestick Press

Published by:
Candlestick Press,
Diversity House, 72 Nottingham Road,
Arnold, Nottingham NG5 6LF
www.candlestickpress.co.uk

Design, typesetting, print and production by Diversity Creative
Marketing Solutions Ltd., www.diversitymarketing.co.uk

Illustrations: © Beth Krommes, 2011
Introduction: © Jenni Murray, 2011

© Candlestick Press, 2011
Reprinted 2012, 2013

ISBN 978 1 907598 09 8

Dedicated to Molly and Billy, the Candlestick Press Pooches.

Acknowledgements:
Candlestick Press thanks Jenni Murray for her Introduction.
Her book *My Boy Butch* is published by Harper Collins and
Butch and Frida can be found in all their photogenic glory on
www.butchthechihuahua.co.uk

Thanks are due to Susan Hamlyn for permission to print 'Attila',
inspired by a real event that happened to the poet Phoebe Hesketh;
to Paul Yandle for 'Dogs', first published in *The North*. 'The Dog'
by Ogden Nash was first printed in *The New Yorker* and is reprinted
by permission of Curtis Brown, Ltd, Copyright © 1957 Ogden Nash.
'Pug' by Stevie Smith is reprinted by kind permission of the Estate of
James MacGibbon; and Siegfried Sassoon, 'Man and Dog', copyright
© Siegfried Sassoon, by kind permission of the Estate of George
Sassoon. Linda Pastan, 'The New Dog' is used by permission of Linda
Pastan in care of the Jean V. Naggar Literary Agency, Inc . 'Another
Reason Why I Don't Keep a Gun in the House' © Billy Collins, 1988,
was first published in *The Apple that Astonished Paris*, The University
of Arkansas Press, 1988, and is reprinted from *Taking Off Emily
Dickinson's Clothes*, Picador, 2000, by kind permission of Billy Collins
and Pan Macmillan.

Where poets are no longer living, their dates are given.

Donation to the Dogs Trust, www.dogstrust.org.uk

Contents   Page

Introduction

For me there was always a dog. As a little girl, before my mother conceded to a gift of the real thing, it was an imaginary Timmy on a string, inspired by Enid Blyton's Famous Five and the adventurous George. Then came Taffy, a corgi cross who became a best friend to a lonely, only child. William and Mary were the miniature schnauzers who grew up with my own children and now there's My Boy Butch - a mini hound who, together with his pal, Frida, has become a substitute for the boys who are now up and off.

People say, 'Jenni Murray....tough, incisive, independent.... going soft in the head over a chihuahua?' They have no idea how a dog can creep into your heart and fill it with utter devotion. No human being greets you with such reliable cheeriness on every occasion or snuggles close to lift your spirits. If I were a poet, I would laud them in exquisite verse, as have those writers included here.

As I write this, Butch is curled up on my bed, Frida alongside him. He appears asleep, but is alive to my every movement, ready to leap up and follow wherever I go. He is brave, loving, kind and hilarious, small as he is. It is not, as they say, the size of the dog in the fight that matters, but the size of the fight in the dog. He would, I know, defend me to the death and all he asks is warmth, food, walkies and my lap for a part of his day.

It's such a relief to find wonderful poems like these and realise you're not alone in your canine passion.

Jenni Murray

Jenni Murray's *My Boy Butch* is published by Harper Collins. Butch's blog can be found on www.butchthechihuahua.co.uk

Epigram Engraved on the Collar of a Dog Which I Gave to His Royal Highness

I am His Highness' dog at Kew;
Pray tell me, sir, whose dog are you?

Alexander Pope (1688 – 1744)

The Dog

The truth I do not stretch or shove
When I state the dog is full of love.
I've also proved, by actual test,
A wet dog is the lovingest.

Ogden Nash (1902 – 1971)

Another Reason Why I Don't Keep a Gun in the House

The neighbors' dog will not stop barking.
He is barking the same high, rhythmic bark
that he barks every time they leave the house.
They must switch him on on their way out.

The neighbors' dog will not stop barking.
I close all the windows in the house
and put on a Beethoven symphony full blast
but I can still hear him muffled under the music,
barking, barking, barking,

and now I can see him sitting in the orchestra,
his head raised confidently as if Beethoven
had included a part for barking dog.

When the record finally ends he is still barking,
sitting there in the oboe section barking,
his eyes fixed on the conductor who is
entreating him with his baton

while the other musicians listen in respectful
silence to the famous barking dog solo,
that endless coda that first established
Beethoven as an innovative genius.

Billy Collins

The New Dog

Into the gravity of my life,
the serious ceremonies
of polish and paper
and pen, has come

this manic animal
whose innocent disruptions
make nonsense
of my old simplicities –

as if I needed him
to prove again that after
all the careful planning,
anything can happen

Linda Pastan

O Pug!

To the Brownes' pug dog, on my lap, in their car,
coming home from Norfolk

O Pug, some people do not like you,
But I like you,
Some people say you do not breathe, you snore,
I don't mind,
One person says he is always conscious of your behind,
Is that your fault?

Your own people love you,
All the people in the family that owns you
Love you: Good pug, they cry, Happy pug,
Pug-come-for-a-walk.

You are an old dog now
And in all your life
You have never had cause for a moment's anxiety,
Yet,
In those great eyes of yours,
Those liquid and protuberant orbs,
Lies the shadow of immense insecurity. There
Panic walks.

Yes, yes, I know,
When your mistress is with you,
When your master
Takes you upon his lap,
Just then, for a moment,
Almost you are not frightened.

But at heart you are frightened, you always have been.

O Pug, obstinate old nervous breakdown,
In the midst of *so* much love,
And such comfort,
Still to feel unsafe and be afraid,

How one's heart goes out to you!

Stevie Smith (1902 – 1971)

Man and Dog

Who's this – alone with stone and sky?
It's only my old dog and I –
It's only him; it's only me;
Alone with stone and grass and tree.

What share we most – we two together?
Smells, and awareness of the weather.
What is it makes us more than dust?
My trust in him; in me his trust.

Here's anyhow one decent thing
That life to man and dog can bring;
One decent thing, remultiplied
Till earth's last dog and man have died.

Siegfried Sassoon (1886 – 1967)

A Dog's Mistake

He had drifted in among us as a straw drifts with the tide,
He was just a wand'ring mongrel from the weary world outside;
He was not aristocratic, being mostly ribs and hair,
With a hint of spaniel parents and a touch of native bear.

He was very poor and humble and content with what he got,
So we fed him bones and biscuits, till he heartened up a lot;
Then he growled and grew aggressive, treating orders with disdain,
Till at last he bit the butcher, which would argue want of brain.

Now the butcher, noble fellow, was a sport beyond belief,
And instead of bringing actions he brought half a shin of beef,
Which he handed on to Fido, who received it as a right
And removed it to the garden, where he buried it at night.

'Twas the means of his undoing, for my wife, who'd stood his friend,
To adopt a slang expression, "went in off the deepest end",
For among the pinks and pansies, the gloxinias and the gorse
He had made an excavation like a graveyard for a horse.

Then we held a consultation which decided on his fate:
'Twas in anger more than sorrow that we led him to the gate,
And we handed him the beef-bone as provision for the day,
Then we opened wide the portal and we told him, "On your way".

Andrew Barton 'Banjo' Paterson (1864 – 1941)

Dogs

Because so many die
before their owners, I wonder
about those few who are left

licking the cold face of the old
woman who falls to the floor,
or prodding a wet nose

into a wheezing bag of ribs,
no voice to call out
or fingers to dial the doctor's number.

I wonder if,
as they circle,
they are thinking of their last meal

or wondering about their next,
and as I offer a corner of toast
I wonder about you –

You,
who we say
would eat anything.

Paul Yandle

Attila Takes A Hand

We drive through the gateway,
Get out of the car
And see to our horror
The door is ajar.

"My God! We've been burgled!
It's happened again!
Perhaps they're still in there?
Bad boys? Or tough men?

"But where is Attila?
Where is that beast?
We thought the Alsatian
Would scare them at least.

"Oh, here is the hero!
And wagging his tail!
Why didn't you give them
Our dinner as well?

"Get back to the kitchen!
Guard dog indeed!
No-one so cowardly
Should wear collar and lead!"

Attila slinks out
But then, strangely, lingers
And sniffs by his forepaw
Two fresh human fingers.

Susan Hamlyn

To Flush, My Dog

Yet, my pretty sportive friend,
Little is't to such an end
That I praise thy rareness!
Other dogs may be thy peers
Haply in these drooping ears,
And this glossy fairness.

But of thee it shall be said,
This dog watched beside a bed
Day and night unweary –
Watched within a curtained room,
Where no sunbeam brake the gloom
Round the sick and dreary.

Roses, gathered for a vase,
In that chamber died apace,
Beam and breeze resigning.
This dog only, waited on,
Knowing that when light is gone
Love remains for shining.

Other dogs in thymy dew
Tracked the hares, and followed through
Sunny moor or meadow.
This dog only, crept and crept
Next a languid cheek that slept,
Sharing in the shadow.

Other dogs of loyal cheer
Bounded at the whistle clear,
Up the woodside hieing.
This dog only, watched in reach
Of a faintly uttered speech,
Or a louder sighing.

And if one or two quick tears
Dropped upon his glossy ears,
Or a sigh came double –
Up he sprang in eager haste,
Fawning, fondling, breathing fast,
In a tender trouble.

And this dog was satisfied
If a pale thin hand would glide
Down his dewlaps sloping –
Which he pushed his nose within,
After platforming his chin
On the palm left open.

Elizabeth Barrett Browning (1806 – 1861)

Inscription on the Monument of a Newfoundland Dog

Near this Spot
are deposited the Remains of one
who possessed Beauty without Vanity,
Strength without Insolence,
Courage without Ferocity,
and all the virtues of Man without his Vices.
This praise, which would be unmeaning Flattery
if inscribed over human Ashes,
is but a just tribute to the Memory of
BOATSWAIN, a DOG
who was born at *Newfoundland* May 1803
and died at *Newstead* Nov 18th 1808.

When some proud son of man returns to earth,
Unknown to glory, but upheld by birth,
The sculptor's art exhausts the pomp of woe,
And storied urns record who rest below:
When all is done, upon the tomb is seen,
Not what he was, but what he should have been:
But the poor dog, in life the firmest friend,
The first to welcome, foremost to defend,
Whose honest heart is still his master's own,
Who labours, fights, lives, breathes for him alone,
Unhonour'd falls, unnoticed all his worth,
Denied in heaven the soul he held on earth –
While man, vain insect! hopes to be forgiven,
And claims himself a sole exclusive heaven.
Oh man! thou feeble tenant of an hour,

Debased by slavery, or corrupt by power,
Who knows thee well must quit thee with disgust,
Degraded mass of animated dust!
Thy love is lust, thy friendship all a cheat,
Thy smiles hypocrisy, thy words deceit!
By nature vile, ennobled but by name,
Each kindred brute might bid thee blush for shame.
Ye! who perchance behold this simple urn,
Pass on – it honours none you wish to mourn:
To mark a friend's remains these stones arise;
I never knew but one, - and here he lies.

Written at Newstead Abbey, November 30, 1808

George Gordon (Lord) Byron (1788 – 1824)